MW00875459

SMALL TOWNS, LABRADORS, BARBECUE, BISCUITS, BEER, AND BIBLES

SEAN DIETRICH

ISBN-13: 978-1530629626

ISBN-10: 1530629624

DEDICATION

If I had one person to whom I would dedicate my writing, it would be to my mother. She's one of the more eccentric and remarkable folks you'd ever care to meet. And I like to think her and I grew up together.

ACKNOWLEDGMENTS

To all the people who read my writings every morning on Facebook, or my blog, thank you. It is because of your support and love that I'm even taking the time to compile these stories into book format. I'll be honest, words fail me. So I'll just say, thanks. And thank you once again.

CORNBREAD

To this day, I've never had two batches of cornbread that were alike. Things like cornbread and biscuits, are the unique fingerprints of a good cook.

My mother made hers using cornmeal, butter, flour, butter, sugar, butter, baking powder, butter, and unsalted butter. Then, she'd scald the bottom of the cornbread until it was dark brown, and serve it with fried chicken livers. Always with chicken livers. My father and I would come to blows over the last remaining liver, and the last piece of cornbread.

The way my mother-in-law makes her cornbread is totally different. She adds jalapenos, onions, and cheese, thereby transforming it in to an homenaje Mexicano. My brother-in-law and I come to blows over that last piece.

My grandmother took a traditional approach. She made her cornbread the old-fashioned way. She prepared it in a rectangular pan that had miniature corncob-shaped sectionals. When it finished baking, she'd pile the muffins into a serving bowl. The strips of caramel-colored cornbread tasted like a delectable mixture of Crisco and the incarnated Jesus Christ.

And no cornbread conversation would be complete without discussing the way my aunt made her cornbread. Here's how she did it: first, we'd hop into her old

Cadillac. Then, we'd ride up to a soul food cafe on the other side of Clayton County, Georgia. She'd bust through the front doors and say, "Hey, y'all got any that cornbread left?"

To which they'd usually reply, "Psssht, girl, make your own cornbread." Then, they'd send us away with an entire box of cornbread, collards, butterbeans.

And a small box of chicken livers for her chubby nephew.

MY FRIEND PATRICK

When I was sixteen, my mother left our town for Atlanta. She was gone three weeks, visiting my aunt while I stayed behind at home. I had the whole house to myself. In the mornings, I fed goats and chickens. In the daytime, I fished for small mouth bass. For supper, I ate Hamburger Helper and watched Abbot and Costello movies. I went weeks without speaking to a soul – except for Mother's phone calls.

It was glorious.

Once, at two in the morning, I awoke to banging on the kitchen door. It scared the bejesus out of me. I flew downstairs to see my friend Patrick behind the screen door. Patrick, who was my age, had driven his truck through our adjoining fields and parked right on top mother's garden. And it's a good thing Mother wasn't there, she would've strung him up by his tongue for that.

I could see Patrick was crying. I opened the screen door. "What's wrong, Pat?"

"My dad," Patrick said. "H-h-he's left my mom. They're getting divorced, I just got in the truck and started driving."

My heart sank. I didn't know what to do. Boys don't cry in front of each other like that. It's against the rules. All I could think to do was fire up the kitchen stove. And

3

that's exactly what I did. I cooked pancakes, bacon, eggs, sausage, grits, and hash browns. We ate until we were good and sick.

I wish I would've known what to say to Pat during that situation. Something compassionate and wise. But I was only sixteen.

And all I knew how to do was make pancakes.

SUNDAY BRUNCHES

"In Alabama," said my father-in-law. "Everybody ate big Sunday lunches, especially in Brewton. It's how things were done. We all gathered at Mother and Daddy's for a big Sunday meal."

Jim stood behind the pot of oyster stew, stirring to keep the butter and milk from burning. I stood watching him, wearing a look on my face I refer to as my *lazy-but-poised* look.

"I don't think anyone has after-church lunches anymore," Jim said. "They're gone. A thing of the past. Young folks have quit such things."

"Well what do people do then?" I asked.

"I don't know, but they sure as hell don't go home and cook." He tapped the spoon on the pot. "I reckon, after church, they lay down and watch FOX News."

"But Jim, you watch FOX News."

"You're missing the point." Jim looked at me. He was fixing to preach. "People in big towns go to big churches, they go to big Walmarts, they send phone text messages." He pointed at my cellphone. "I don't even know what a text is."

5

I silently thanked the Lord for that.

"Shoot," he said. "Doctors don't even come to anyone's houses anymore. We've gotten so big that you and I are nothing but numbers, nowadays."

"What does any of that have to do with anything?"

"It has everything to do with everything. Because, nobody eats together anymore. Nobody cooks big Sunday meals – with gravy. We've gotten too big. People don't visit after church."

"But Jim," I said. "You cook every Sunday, and we're always here."

"I'm not talking about you," he scoffed. "You're just a lazy-ass looking for free food."

FAST LEARNER

The first thing I remember teaching my sister, after she learned to tie her shoes, was how to make bacon. She stood on a chair in front of the stove while I demonstrated fatback frying in the iron skillet. I also taught her how to dry it with paper towels, and how to save her bacon grease in a coffee can.

It only took one lesson at the stovetop. She took to frying bacon like a skink takes to a garage. And as the weeks went on, she prepared bacon twice per day, every day – so help me God.

She'd fry up an entire skillet of it and split it with me. We ate so much bacon I had to wear a T-shirt to the public pool. And I sunk straight to the bottom whenever I tried to go swimming. My towheaded little sister helped me gain nine pounds in two weeks.

Finally, I explained to her that people don't eat this much bacon, and certainly never after breakfast.

"But," she said. "What about BLTs?"

"Well, those are different, BLTs are a summer thing."

"What about Hoppin' John, or pinto beans? They

7

have bacon, and they're not breakfast foods."

I shrugged. "Well, I guess you're right."

Satisfied with her own reasoning, my sister went to the icebox. I stopped her. "No, no." I yanked the fatback away. "Look, if you want bacon for supper, I'm going to teach you how to combine it with something healthy, like a responsible American."

"A salad?" she asked.

"Close, I'm going to teach you how to make a bacon cheeseburger."

TACO BELL

I've never met a person I didn't like – until today. Her name was Edna, and she's from Minnesota. I don't know anything about Minnesotans, except that they use firewood and talk like they have perpetual head colds.

I saw Edna somewhere outside Gulf Breeze, in a Taco Bell parking lot with a flat tire. It's not every day you see a white-haired woman trying to change her own tire. I pulled alongside and offered to help.

"No," Edna said. "I don't need help, don't cha know."

Don't cha know?

I refused to take no for an answer. I nudged her out of the way, explaining that my mother was Lutheran. That seemed to satisfy Edna, who is also Lutheran. She understood no self-respecting mother would forgive her son for overlooking a hapless Lutheran at the Taco Bell.

While I worked, Edna explained she was no ordinary Lutheran, she'd been a widow since the age of thirty. She never remarried, but raised three God-fearing Minnesotans who still live there today.

Edna said, "Last year, I decided Minnesota was too

dagnabbin' cold. I wanted to live in Florida, where I could get a decent sunburn."

"Don't cha know," I added.

Edna relocated to Pensacola Beach. She owns a condo right on the water. She wakes up every morning to the Gulf, and goes to sleep with her bedroom windows open, listening to the surf. She likes living here. And in her own words, "Good riddance, Minnesota. If my kids need me, they can text me."

And it was then I realized I didn't like Edna.

I love her.

BOILED PEANUTS

The first time I ate a boiled green peanut I was eight years old, in Mamers, North Carolina. My first reaction was joy, followed by more joy. How could I have gone my entire life without knowing about boiled peanuts? I was practically middle-aged.

By the time I was in my twenties, I'd developed a full-blown addiction. I looked for excuses to ride past a small roadside peanut stand. I'd sit on the back of my tailgate and eat cajun peanuts until I ruptured something or passed out. Whichever came first.

Of course, boiled peanuts go with college football, beer – and beer. I experienced my first Alabama-Auburn fight over a bowl of hot boiled peanuts. It was at a small place of business in Holmes County, Florida. It went like this:

The Iron Bowl played on an enormous bar room television. Auburn scored.

One Alabama fan shouted, "!@#$% Auburn!" The man was about as loaded as a potato gun at the time.

Just then, another man shot up on the other side of

the bar, wearing navy and orange. "What'd you say?" He said, slurring every word of it.

A full-on fight broke out. Boiled peanuts went flying everywhere. One vision viscerally singed into my memory happened when the Alabama fan crawled atop the bar. He dropped his jeans and mooned the entire establishment. He shouted, "Roooooww tadd!" Then shook his hindquarters from side to side. Immediately, his Auburn adversary grabbed a handful of peanuts and wriggled up onto the bar beside him.

Auburn won. Seven to seventeen.

THANK GOD FOR TWINKIES

I thank God for Twinkies. Why? Because before folks knew what yoga was, before anyone used words like, "eating clean," or "Donald Trump," we ate golden spongecake from Hostess. And we ate it because it made us feel better. It was part of growing up, a comfort food. Nobody told us Twinkies were Satanic.

But I guess they are.

Likewise, nobody told us growing up would be so hard, either. But it was. The process of becoming an adult is bone-stretching difficult. There's no roadmap for it, and there's no way of knowing when you're past Twinkie-age.

At thirteen, my legs grew so fast my muscles and tendons couldn't keep up. I laid in bed and cried from the aches. It made me walk funny. Much like a penguin who'd just ridden a stallion across the Sierra mountains. During this period – one I'd like to forget – they called me Corncob.

I went through another phase of life when I was as uncoordinated as a cinder block. Overnight, I turned into a bumbling idiot. Whenever someone lobbed a football at me, I'd flail through the air like an elephant wearing blue jeans.

Still, the hardest part was the mental challenge of growing up. No matter who you were, popular or unpopular, it was hard. I don't know anyone who didn't struggle; who didn't feel ugly, who didn't wish God would've made them taller, slimmer, or better-looking.

You want to know why I still like Twinkies?

Because it doesn't get any easier as an adult.

THE POLITE ONES

"Dear," she said to her husband. "Would you mind getting the car while I wait here?"

Her husband was a short, white-haired man who might've weighed a-buck-ten, sopping wet. He nodded his head. "I don't mind, darling, but I'll be awhile." He pointed to the edge of the Publix parking lot. "We parked way out there."

She sat down on the bench and laid her purse in her lap. "I'll stay here with the groceries, you get the car, if you don't have any objections."

He rubbed her arthritic shoulders. "I don't mind. Whatever you want, dear."

The elderly couple shared a moment of polite affection. Something that struck me as quite remarkable this day in age.

"Please be careful, Harold," she said. "Watch for traffic."

"Honey." He removed his crimson-colored Alabama cap. "I'll be as safe as I can." Then, he leaned down and pecked her on the cheek. "Give me a few minutes and I'll return."

And he hobbled out toward their car.

I'll be honest with you, I'm not sure what's happened to our world. Couples don't treat each other with this kind of politeness. Not anymore. We thumb-type on our cellphones, we use swear words like they're Morton salt. Furthermore, when young couples are in the supermarket, you don't find many using words like, "please," or "thank you."

Just then, a car swerved and laid on the horn. The old man jogged across the intersection barely dodging the erratic vehicle.

The old man held up an ugly finger and shouted, "Watch where you're going! You @%#ing piece of $#!+"

FIXING THE SINK

"My mother had a pet mule," said my mother-in-law. "Outside Brewton, when she was a little girl. She named him Henry."

While my mother-in-law talked, I laid beneath her bathroom sink with a wrench in hand. She watched me struggle, unclogging thirty-seven-year's worth of slimy hair that smelled like trout poop.

Mary droned on. "My mother would ride her mule..."

"Miss Mary, would you hand me the pliers?"

"But the mule wouldn't walk in straight lines..."

"Pliers, if you please?"

"The mule only walked in circles..."

"Never mind." I stood up holding a handful of fetid hair clumps.

"Then, one day," Mary ignored me. "My mother decided she didn't want to ride in circles. So..."

I flushed the foul-smelling bile down the toilet, gagged, then made the sign of the cross.

"Don't you want to know what happened next?" Mary asked.

"I'm dying to know," I mumbled.

"Well, you see..."

I crawled underneath the sink to remove another helping of mephitic sludge from the drainpipe.

Mary continued. "Then, Mother and her mule..."

By this time, I was paying no attention to Mary's story. I shot to my feet, hacking and spitting. My face was covered in what looked like something a well-hydrated two-year-old squeezes into his diaper.

"What's the matter?" Mary asked.

"The matter," I shot back, "is that I just got that radioactive diarrhea in my mouth."

"Oh." Mary shrugged. "Well, does this mean you aren't going to put my mule story in your next book?"

"Miss Mary, it's just..." I let out a colossal sigh and wiped the filth from my face. "Of course I am."

BUTTERMILK OF SOURDOUGH

I visited Santa Claus at Weaver's department store as a child. When he asked me what I'd like, I told him matter-of-factly, "Biscuits." He gave me a funny look and asked if I wanted anything else. I shrugged. "Well, maybe some syrup."

That Christmas, I got a jar of sorghum syrup.

My mother believed biscuits to be medicinal. Not Pilsbury biscuits, but homemade on the countertop. Buttermilk, angel, sourdough, and drop biscuits; served with soft butter and sorghum syrup.

When I fell out of our mulberry tree and fractured my arm, mother made cathead biscuits. She made mulberry jam to go with them, just to be funny. When our baseball team won regionals, Daddy bought a box of fried chicken. I sat on his tailgate and did what I always did; I ate the biscuits first.

And even at Daddy's funeral, there were more biscuits than I could shake a stick at. One individual even brought a paper sack full of buttermilk biscuits and honey – and wrote my name on the bag.

I never found out who did that.

When I graduated, Mother made drop biscuits. When a girl broke my heart, I drove two hours just to eat biscuits at a truck-stop. At our first apartment, a nearby diner served sourdough biscuits so fluffy they were illegal in six states. I could eat nine. This week alone, I've eaten biscuits on Sunday, Tuesday, Wednesday, and Thursday. In fact, I'm eating one right now.

I don't know what it is about biscuits.

And I don't care.

TAG

Playing tag is a terrible game. I wouldn't wish a round of tag on my worst enemy. You remember how it goes: when a player is touched, that person is "it." And if that child is nonathletic, he will be marked for the rest of his life.

Consequently, I've been "it" since the eighties.

The last time I was tagged was when I was a child. I remember it was a beautiful autumn because my grandfather was smoking a pork butt at the time. He usually barbecued during the fall. He'd smoke pork butts, pork shoulders, ribs, and anything else that had a pulse. He cooked his meat low and slow until it fell off the bone.

He'd begin the process early in the mornings. After bathing the pork in mustard and paprika, he'd place it over smoldering hickory chips. Then, he'd shut the lid and remain in that little chair until supper. He'd puff a cigarette, drink coffee, and tell inappropriate jokes to slow-running freckled boys who'd been tagged "it."

I was one such boy.

That day, I collapsed beside my grandfather from physical exhaustion.

"Why're you breathing so heavy?" he asked.

"I can't catch those kids," I said, panting. "And I'm it."

"It?"

"I'm a slow runner."

My grandfather thought for a moment. He lifted the lid of the smoker and pinched a sliver of meat to test it. Then, he handed a small piece to me.

When I ate it, I let out a ceremonious moan.

"There," he said. "That's what you get for being 'it.'"

Well.

Maybe tag wasn't so bad after all.

EXACT CHANGE

I don't know why it was so hard for me to understand one thing: that everything changes. Such basics seem like common knowledge, but it hasn't always been that clear for me.

As a boy I didn't know the world changed like it did. That things change. That life changes. That life changes people. That people die. Or perhaps I should say it how my grandfather would say it, "I'm afraid change is here to stay, boy."

I suppose he was right. Babies change. Kids change. Teenagers change schools, friends, jobs. Twenty-year-olds trying to discover themselves change points of view. Thirty-year-olds with identity problems change careers. Fifty-year-olds change hairstyles, they divorce their old Cadillac then upgrade to a new wife. Seventy-year-olds change life-roles, then they change ideals. Eighty-year-olds just miss their friends.

But I do believe there's an exception to the rule:

Peanut butter.

Peanut butter does not change. It stays the same. I ate

a peanut butter sandwich yesterday; it tasted the same as always. Thick, robust, and capable of choking you to death. Another exception: cheese. Cheese does not change. Each slice of cheese I've ever had eats the same as it did when I was knee-high.

The list goes on and on. Beer. Beer tastes the same as it did when I was a five-year-old on my daddy's knee. The taste of a tomato doesn't change – thank God. Ice cream sandwiches, they don't change. Neither do apple fritters, mashed potatoes, cajun pork rinds, Captain Crunch, oyster crackers, Twinkies, Heinz ketchup, beef jerky, Bazooka bubblegum, whole milk, or sourwood honey, fresh from Robertsdale, Alabama.

Or love.

THE RAIN

The rain used to drive my father crazy. He hated the idea of being trapped indoors; especially when there was work to do outside. And there was always work to do, he'd never let anyone forget it.

On rainy days we did the same thing. My father would read the paper on the porch and complain about feeling as useless as "tits on a boar." My mother would sit on the swing, knitting something for somebody's baby. And we'd just watch the rain fall.

The sound of rain on forty acres is deafening.

Occasionally, my father would put down his paper and just stare. He'd shake his head from time to time and say, "Dammit, I had a lot to do today." But I don't think he meant a word of it – not really. I think he liked the break.

Sometimes, we'd sit out there for the entire day. Mother would make sandwiches for lunch. Daddy would wolf one down, still reading the paper and say, "I wish this rain would let up."

And nobody answered him.

For the life of me, I never figured out why we sat outside on rainy days like that. My mother told me once, "It's because we grew up without air conditioning. It's just what people do. Watch the rain fall."

But, you know what I think? I don't think it has anything to do with air conditioning. Because I've got all the air conditioning I can stand. I've also got satellite television, three computers, fast internet, and a cellphone smarter than me.

And yesterday, I just sat on the porch.

KEEGO

If you've been to my house, then you've seen the cattails by my front door. And you've probably asked about them, too. A big bouquet of them sit on our porch. They've been there for years now.

Anyone who has ever fished in a little pond knows all about cattails. Because that's where they often grow.

The cattails on my porch come from Keego, Alabama. A place my wife's family has lived for ten billion generations, dating all the way back to the Creek Indian tribes. Though Jamie swears she has no Creek blood in her, when the sun comes out to play she sure browns like one.

Keego is not a town. It's not a city either. It's a minuscule community in the woods with railroad tracks and a church. The pond there isn't big enough to hold more than a few small mouth bass and a couple bullfrogs. And whenever you pile into the little fishing skiff, the pond level rises a whole foot.

My father-in-law fished this small water all his life. He fished it with his own father, mother, brothers, sisters, preacher, wife, children, and even his freeloading son-in-law.

Yours truly.

He'd spend an entire afternoon in that little skiff, only seventy feet from shore. Sometimes, he wouldn't catch anything but a sunburn and a pissy attitude. He'd float in those cattails like he was angry at the fish, spitting out cuss words. Like a Creek Indian with a quick temper and a sailor's mouth. But he wasn't mad, not at all. He was content. Because Brother Jim was an Alabamian.

And cattails did that to him.

READ THE INSTRUCTIONS

When we first got engaged, the minister refused to marry us until we read an instructional book. The books cost a cool sixty dollars each. The reverend recommended we buy two. So, I put mine on layaway.

Jamie and I became dedicated matrimonial students. We completed our marriage homework every Monday, Wednesday, and Friday. I learned basic marital skills I might never have learned with other twenty-dollar books.

For instance: the book recommended using the phrase, "How's your love account, honey?" The partner responds by attaching a dollar amount to the level of spousal intimacy. I once asked Jamie how her account was. She told me I'd overdrafted twice and made us late on the electric bill. Then, she confiscated my wallet and cut up my debit cards.

Another book admonishment: men are microwaves and women are ovens. Meaning, men anger and cool down fast; women take their time doing both. Whoever wrote that never met my wife because she's neither. I'd liken her to a stovetop pressure cooker full of tomato puree. Just yesterday, I asked Jamie if she'd kindly quiet the damn vacuum while I watched baseball – for my love account.

Now, I'm covered in what look like rug burns.

More book advice: hold hands while arguing. This one is marvelous for young couples. Especially when one of you is a pressure cooker. Once, during a disagreement on a road trip, I attempted to hold Jamie's hand. At first, it seemed to work. She quit talking. Then, she smiled, pulled the car over, and left me for dead in Milton, Florida.

I would've called a cab, but she'd frozen my love account.

ONE OCTOBER DAY

When my father first died, I wouldn't come out of my room for nearly three weeks. I stayed locked inside. I laid on my bed and stared at the ceiling. I did a lot of crying and listening to Daddy's records. Hank Williams, and the immortal George Jones.

After a month of this, my mother decided it was time for me to join the human race. One October day, my mother pounded on my door.

I didn't answer.

"Please open the door, honey," she said.

Still no answer.

"I have a present for you."

She knew how to get my attention.

When I opened the door, my mother was cradling something in her arms. Something furry, only three pounds. It was pitch black with tan patches.

I named her Hannah.

I wish I could tell you all about Hannah, but there's too much to say. I wouldn't be able to find the right words. I can't describe how she followed me in the woods when I'd attempt to hunt dove. Or how she'd lead the way back when I returned empty-handed. About how Hannah sat by my feet while I fished, eating my earthworms like spaghetti. How she hated fetch, peed like a weirdo, or slept with her head in the crook of my armpit.

I wouldn't be able to tell you how she hated to see my cry, how she'd lick me until I laughed, or how her breath smelled like the wrong side of a goat. Neither can I tell you how it grieved me when she finally went deaf and blind. Or how blurry my eyes were when I dug her grave.

I'm sorry, I just can't seem to find the words.

CARL

I met Carl at a Freeport gas station. He was driving a Ford truck, same year, make, and model as mine. The same color, too; I call it, cold sore red. We were twins. The only difference between our vehicles was that Carl's sat loaded with a metric ton of fresh hickory. He had so many logs, it looked like his axel was going to buckle under the weight.

"Nice truck," I said.

He gave me a grin. "Not half as cute as yours."

I looked back at my vehicle. It looked like last year's runner-up in the ugly contest.

"Why so much wood?" I asked.

"Hickory," he answered. "It's for my dad. I drove four hours to get all this free wood. Craigslist."

Carl and his father own a barbecue joint in middle Georgia. A small one. Nearly a decade ago, they were barbecue gods. They did battle in slow cook-offs all over the Southeast with nothing but an iron smoker, a few pork shoulders, and sass. Not only did they win contests, they helped pork addicts like me expand waistlines one mouthful at a time.

"Dad will go nuts over all this free hickory," Carl explained. Then, his face grew solemn. "He's got Alzheimers now. It makes every day a challenge."

Carl showed me an old photograph of his father. The two of them stood before a big smoker with medals dangling from their necks. Arms wrapped around each other's shoulders. Then, Carl bid me goodbye. Because middle Georgia is a long way from Freeport.

And Carl had a special delivery to make.

PUDGY

As a boy, they nicknamed me Biscuit. It wasn't just because I loved biscuits –though I most certainly did. It was because my waistline stayed in a consistent state of jolliness. And to top it off, my mother often made me wear a pair of absurd red suspenders to school.

Finally, at the age of twelve, Mother tried to help me lose weight. She put me on the Atkin's Diet. It was awful, like living in a biscuitless purgatory. She fed me chicken breasts, cabbage, and the worst concoction God ever allowed on His earth: skim milk. It was during this period I took to hiding candy in my underpants. My buddy avowed that M&M's only melted in one's mouth, but he was wrong.

Very wrong.

Mother also tried to motivate me to exercise. She made me walk an entire mile to the bus stop each morning. Such nonsense lasted for exactly one day before I discovered the illicit joys of skipping school.

When my diet ended, thanks to M&M's and Moonpies, I clocked in at two pounds heavier than my original weight. My father assured me the problem was genetic. "I was chubby, too," he said. "So was my daddy. We were all fluffy."

Fluffy?

To prove it, Daddy rifled through an old shoebox of photographs. He handed me a picture of a round child with cropped hair. The boy was identical to me, minus the Santa Claus suspenders and chocolaty drawers.

I hung my head. "Daddy, they call me Biscuit."

"Well," he said. "That's just flat-out ridiculous. You're no Biscuit."

"I'm not?"

"No. You're Biscuit Junior."

JESSIE

This week, my friend Jessica completes her GED. That might not sound impressive to you, but it is to me.

Jessica was a sweetheart. Not my sweetheart, she was too much of a tomboy for that. No, Jessie was one of the fellas. If you looked past her skinned knees and foul mouth, you'd see a girl.

She was tough; good at shooting, climbing trees, telling jokes, and spitting. And she could cram more tobacco into her mouth than any boy I ever knew and not get sick.

This, I learned the hard way.

Since birth, Jessie show-jumped horses. I watched her practice on the back of her farm. She'd whip Softy into a canter and leap over the arrowheads. Then, she'd turn Softy around and stride over taller fence-combinations.

And leave us boys speechless.

At age fifteen, something happened to Jessie. She started getting nauseated in the mornings. Things got worse. After a few months, Jessica's clothes weren't fitting. Her face got puffy, and her pants became tight. It didn't take long to figure out what was happening inside of her little body.

In her eighteenth week of pregnancy, they expelled Jessie. She never came back, and nobody treated her the same afterward. Small-town people can be downright vicious when they want to be.

Well, I never gave a blessed damn what they thought of Jessie. I didn't back then, and I sure as hell don't now. If you ask me, a thirty-three-year-old girl with a GED can prove a lot of judgmental, closet-drinking Baptists wrong. Congratulations, Jessie darling.

Give that daughter of yours a kiss.

CHEROKEES

My mother decided to grow tomatoes in September, she got the idea after reading a book Daddy bought her on indoor gardening. She set up shop in the basement and planted her heirloom seeds in galvanized washtubs. A huge fluorescent lamp hung over them, along with a painted a sign reading, "Do not touch my tomatoes or I will castrate you. Love, Mom."

After several weeks, the tomato plants sprouted and began producing fruit. The dark Cherokee heirlooms were the same color as the ones Mother grew in her summer gardens. And so, each morning, she'd pick ripe tomatoes and hoard them away. If she ever caught Daddy or me pilfering her stash, she'd neuter us with a dull spoon before we could count to three.

One night, Daddy came home late after a football game. He was staggering like he had vertigo, slurring his words. He snuck into my room and woke me up quietly. "Ssshh," he said, smelling like Wild Turkey and cigars. "Come down to the kitchen, let's eat some damn supper. What do you say?"

He didn't have to ask twice.

Supper is exactly what we did. Together, we ate honest-to-goodness tomato sandwiches in December. He ate three, I ate two. We made them with Mother's homemade bread and slaps of Duke's mayonnaise.

Then the kitchen light flipped on.

We shielded our loins.

Mother yanked the sandwich from Daddy and said, "You drunk idiot." Then, she took a big bite, leaving a streak of mayo on her cheek. She took another bite. Then another. And then another.

Castration would have to wait.

IN ANOTHER TIME

I never heard my grandfather use a swear word around women. Nothing more than, "hell," or an occasional "dammit," – which weren't considered swear words. To him, gasoline was measured in cents, not dollars. Playboy wasn't a magazine, but a nickname grandma called him when he gambled at the horse track.

And one of my favorite things was how he referred to females of any age; darling or sweetie.

He owned the same car for twenty-one years, an Opel. His DeSoto, even longer. He never saw the internet. To him, a computer was a human mathematician in the United States Army. He wore his nicest clothes to baseball games, stood for the National Anthem, and by God, we put hands over hearts. This was the only moment in a man's life permissible for shedding tears.

A text message was something read aloud on Sunday mornings by a minister. Cellphones were devices used in prison. Back then, there existed no touchscreens. In fact, you never touched the television screen, especially not before Hee Haw.

Highway speeds over fifty-five were speeding. If your wife was pregnant, you got a cigar – and you smoked it right then and there. Sunglasses were for wise guys. Drugs came from a corner pharmacy, and pot was what you cooked oyster stew in. There were no twenty-four-hour news channels, because there was no such thing as good news anyway. Well – except for V-Day and the book of Matthew. The world has changed. For the better? I don't know, and I don't care.

Because he would've found a way to be happy here, too.

MICHAEL

My father's friend Michael died last week. Michael had one arm. Well technically, he had one and a half arms. His right arm was missing from the elbow down.

Whenever Michael would come to our house, he would say something like, "Don't ever scratch a mosquito bite, or you'll end up like this." Or he might say, "If you shake hands with a woman of the night, her sin will eat up your arm."

I asked Mother what women of the night were.

"Girls who don't eat all their broccoli," she said.

Of course the real story was Michael lost his arm as a teenager. It happened one night while Daddy and Michael were riding the county roads. They were no doubt tight as a couple of ticks. While Daddy drove, Michael shoved his arm out the speeding passenger window to grab a handful of daisies growing tall near the roadside.

For a girl.

Daddy rode as close to the ditch as he could. Michael reached out and came up empty handed. He tried again.

But it was dark. And Michael didn't see the fencepost.

Daddy once told me he had three regrets in his life. Michael's right arm, not going to college, and I never learned the third. But Michael held no grudges. At my father's funeral Michael told me, "Your daddy was the best damn friend I ever had." Michael used his hook to wipe his eyes and said, "I'd give my good arm to have him back." But as it turns out, there was no need.

Because now Michael has his friend and his arms.

FEAR

If I could remove something from this world, it would be fear. I hate it. And it comes in a billion different shapes and colors. Sometimes, it looks like Jehovah's Witnesses, or cellphone bills. Sometimes, it looks like Jim Cantore.

But I'm not talking about little things like spiders, snakes, or rats. I'm talking about the hard stuff. Fear of rejection, of loneliness, or failure.

When I was a toddler, no one explained adults feel more fear than children do. But it's true. And it only gets worse the older you become. First, I was afraid of bad grades, hot-tempered brunettes, and gym shorts. Now, I'm starting to fear things like unqualified barbers who text while they cut hair, and I still fear hot-tempered brunettes.

And, the biggest shame is that we don't talk enough about the things that make us less afraid. About the tokens that take the sting out of being alive.

I wish kids heard more about miracles, about Claude Monet, John Wayne, Merel Haggard, and dolphins. That every child could taste buckwheat honey, or ride a horse – just once. To know that puppies are our greatest gifts; that God made Conecuh County, Alabama smoked sausage with His own two hands; that hide-and-seek is more important than straight A's; that it's always appropriate to shout "kick his ass!" during a football game; that kissing is as good as life will ever get; that humans are capable of real love. That we don't have to be afraid.

That things will be okay.

That everything will be okay.

No matter what.

FRIDAYS

When we first got married, Fridays represented our date night, the highlight of our week. One evening, after work, Jamie asked me, "Honey britches, where do you want to eat tonight?"

I answered, "I don't know peach blossom."

"I want steak," Jamie said, adjusting the strap on her shoes.

When we arrived at the steakhouse, Jamie had changed her mind. So, we tried Chinese. But she'd changed her mind again. "I'm not in the mood for Asian tonight, sugar binky." By the sixth restaurant, Jamie's blood sugar had already sunk to a dangerous low. She assumed a pissy, matter-of-fact voice. "I want seafood, that's what I want."

We loaded into the car and headed for seafood. While waiting for a table at the crab shack, the flower of my existence said, "I don't want to eat here. Their fish smells fishy." I kindly pointed out that fish, by its very nature, is fishy – as opposed to say, chickeny. Jamie popped me in the mouth like a toddler who'd just sassed his mother.

We tried the pizza joint. But Jamie decided she hated, olive oil, bread, cheese, and the state of Florida. We tried the Mediterranean restaurant. Jamie wasn't about to eat a shish-ka-nothing. We tried Mexican, Thai, sushi, Hungarian, and even infallible Barbecue. Nothing suited her. By two in the morning, I had a black eye, my new nickname was Greasy Prick, and we still hadn't settled on a place.

"You know," Jamie finally said. "Just go wherever you want, $#*!-for-brains. I'm not even hungry."

So, I did what I felt right.

I bought a gallon of ice cream and a six-pack.

LEFT FIELD

I was a terrible centerfielder, but I wasn't half as bad as our left-fielder, Charlie. He was god-awful. He threw the ball like his arm was only half-attached at the shoulder.

When we were sixteen, Charlie and I lost a regional championship for our team together. The coach called us Abbot and Costello because neither of us ever knew "who the hell was on first."

The end of Charlie's sports career came when he began fraternizing with the wrong crowd of people. Sometimes, he'd come to practice looking like the bottom of a horse hoof, half-hungover. Still drunk.

I remember the day the coach cut him from the team. Because that day, Charlie smelled like vodka and cigarettes. He started crying in front of the whole team and promised to clean up his act.

But he didn't.

Eventually, Charlie dropped out of school. Then, he started using stuff a lot harder than vodka, and living in his car. He got down to ninety pounds, and gossips rumored that he'd died of an overdose.

Well, it's been thirteen years, and Charlie is anything but dead.

The last time I saw Charlie, he was a different man. Clean as the preacher's sheets. Sober as a house cat. "It was my uncle," Charlie said. "He saved me. Took me to meetings. He and my aunt fed me – from their own table."

Charlie looks good. He can bench press quadruple digits, he doesn't drink, doesn't smoke, and he's happy to tell you about it. And even though, Charlie probably still throws like a girl; I know the truth.

He's the most superb left-fielder I ever knew.

CORY

His name was Cory, and he hated the water. He wasn't like any of my other friends, he was different. And back then, people didn't use words like autism. Ignorant people used harsh words, ones not fit to use on labradors.

Cory and I weren't exactly close. But then, there's no way we could've been, he never used more than one-syllable sentences. Still, he remembered every insignificant thing you ever said or did. And he'd log such marginal information away for future use against you, should the need arise. Cory was happy to spend time with us boys, as long as it didn't involve water.

Water terrified him.

One day, several of us fished the "fork," where the creek met the river. Cory didn't want to drink beer with us, he was too smart for that, and he certainly didn't go near the water. So, Cory sat at a far distance while we fished.

Well, it didn't take long for our pal Andrew to do something stupid, as was his custom. That day, Andy staggered into the water to chase a catfish. He was immediately swept away by the current. Which wouldn't have been life threatening if Andy were sober – but he wasn't.

In an instant, Cory kicked his shoes off, and leapt into the water. He swam out a ways and pulled a very drunk Andy to shore with an incredible display of strength.

Cory yelled. "I've got you Andy! You're going to live a long, long life!"

And as far as I know, Andy is living a long life – and married, too.

Because Cory was his best man.

23RD STREET

I'm not a traveller. In fact, I've never been anywhere noteworthy, unless you count Tijuana.

The one time I visited New York City, I had a nervous breakdown on 23rd Street. The embarrassing event happened in front of a place called the Flatiron Building. The doctor said it was a case of shock. He explained that my dizziness would go away when I returned to scenery that vaguely resembled pastures. But the nausea never subsided, I was wobbly for six days.

I've never seen that many people wearing suits in my life, and I've never cared to, either.

See, to understand the rural mediocrity that is me, you ought to know I grew up an hour from town. My friends had horses before driver's licenses. We wore denim and looked stupid in it. We wrung chickens' necks; and we didn't call it farm-to-table, we called it supper. We milked cows and bitched about it, like you're supposed to. We shot rifles at bales of hay. Our parents ate scrambled pork brains and eggs for breakfast and didn't save us any.

We loved liver of all kinds, and so did our dogs. City-folk hated liver, and so did their dogs.

Most of us boys only ever had one good girlfriend. Not because we didn't yearn for more experience, but because there weren't many girls around. We loved our mothers, we ate our vegetables, we said grace before supper, and by God, we watched the World Series.

Whenever we left town, we were sick until we got back.

And the truth is, we still get that way.

THE RIGHT THING

I once lost a wallet with one thousand dollars cash tucked in it. I lost it in a Piggly Wiggly parking lot. The next day, the store called me. They informed me someone had returned my wallet to the front desk along with a yellow sticky note reading, "Do the right thing."

I wish I had that note.

Another time: I had a tire blowout on the highway. A man from the Department of Transportation pulled over to help me change my tire. The whole ordeal ended up taking only ten minutes. I tried to pay him fifty dollars, but he gave an emphatic "no," stating he was a Methodist and didn't accept money for acts of charity. So, the gentleman and I visited the First United Chapel Of The Tom-Thumb-Six-Pack.

After all, he was Methodist.

Here's another story: fourth grade. Grandparent's Day. It was a day when children's grandparents visited them at school. I was the only student in our entire class without a pair of white-haired visitors. I sat at my desk feeling like most lonely little boy on earth. My grandfather was ill, and we'd just recently laid my grandmother in the ground.

That's when my teacher, Mrs. Everhardt, called her husband to pinch hit. Together, she and he served as my surrogate grandparents for the day. She told my classmates she and I were related, distant cousins – which was a blatant lie. Mrs. Everhardt still sends me a card on my birthdays. She signs it, "Grandma."

Don't tell me good people don't exist.

Because I'll bet you a thousand bucks they do.

CHARLIE

Charlie always smelled bad, and he had oily hair. He never bathed, and neither did any of his six sisters or brothers. They were perpetually filthy, their clothes ragged. People looked down on Charlie because his daddy worked in a factory. Charlie's older brothers, who'd all dropped out of school, worked in the same plant.

And that, by God, was life.

I only ever saw Charlie on Sundays. His family would sit in front of my family at church every week. His daddy wore the same outdated suit, and he'd bellow hymns like his hair was on fire. Charlie's quiet mother barely moved her mouth at all to sing. Charlie's older sister, who was far too pretty to be wearing that patched-up dress, would sing while rocking her baby brother on her hip.

Charlie just kept his hands in his pockets.

Even though he was my age, we didn't have anything in common, Charlie and me. His life was different than mine. But I do remember him. And I think about his family often. I wonder how they're getting along. I wonder where they live, or if they bathe. I wonder if his daddy still smokes cigarettes the moment he exits that chapel. I wonder about Charlie's brown-eyed older sister, and if she ever got a new dress. I wonder about Charlie, too. I wonder if his hair is still a little on the greasy side.

I wonder if that college scholarship changed him.

I wonder how it feels to have the same folks who looked down on you, bring you their sick babies and call you, "Doctor."

FIVE THOUSAND FOLKS

I'd like to tell you about a place you might not know, though you might've seen exit signs off Alabama Interstate 65. It's a place with a little over five-thousand folks, and an IGA.

If you look closer, you'll see it's a place where beer joints still exist. A town where football isn't televised, it's practiced. A fleck on the map, where the main religion is family; secondary only to hospitality and chicken salad. Here, people spend afternoons on their porches, watching traffic. And every year, they get excited about something called the Blueberry Festival.

It is the only place where I am recognized in the supermarket only by my wife's maiden name.

The American Sabbath is still Sunday here, and always will be. Hard work is the only profession there is, and God-fearing ladies only skip Bible study when they have a nagging case of yellow fever. Women still wear dresses; and nobody gives a flavored fruit-salad how folks dress in L.A.

Biscuits are heavy, beer is light, and sweet tea is

sugary enough to break your cotton-picking jaw.

It's a place where engagement parties involve half the population. Where it's permissible to plan weddings around the SEC calendar. Where people tell a dumb redheaded groom he's part of their family, even though he's a stranger. The same idiot redhead who has no idea what in God's name he's signed up for. They shake his hand, feed him slow-cooked pork, and they call him "son."

All five damn thousand of them.

The name of the town doesn't matter.

THE ALABAMIAN

"My name is El Charrito de Alabama," said Esteban. "But you can call me Steve."

I shook Esteban's hand and noticed it felt strange and rough, like a dried baseball mitt. When I looked at it closely, I saw he was missing fingers. Esteban told me he lost those fingers at age twelve, in an accident involving an axe, a cruel boss, and the man's daughter. Something else you ought to know about Esteban: he's famous.

As a teenager, the rodeo came to his village and discovered the orphan cowboy twirling a lasso with his mangled hand. He could rope anything that had the gall to move. Including rabbits and rattle snakes who'd been de-rattled.

The rodeo finally landed him in Alabama. He's lived there ever since, as a naturalized citizen. At first, he didn't speak much English. He could only say basic phrases like, "thank you," or "you're welcome." But now he can say things like, "Two Hardee's chicken biscuits, please," like a bonafide Southerner. Esteban also uses words like "y'all," and they sound funny with his thick-tongued accent. But after forty years as an Alabama resident, such words are his God-given right.

No one recognizes Esteban as a famous vaquero, to most he's just a faceless Mexican with a deformed hand. But Esteban becomes something more when he picks up his lasso. And he drops thirty years. Then, he tosses the lasso over my head and tightens it around my waist. And for a moment, he's not a lonesome, five-foot-two field worker with a screwed-up hand.

He's Esteban, El Charrito de Alabama.

But you can call him Steve.

FRENCH FRIES

"Frozen French fries are a disgrace," my mother used to say while hand-slicing potatoes. "Real fries aren't hard to make, why do people buy frozen ones? They taste like salted cotton."

Mother knew how much I loved fries. And whenever she made fresh-cut shoestrings, I knew they were just for me. It didn't matter who requested them, or how many she made. If Mother fried Russet potatoes in an iron skillet, they were intended for Sean Paul Dietrich Senior.

Once, Mother tried to teach me how to make fries, but it was disastrous. I was an awful potato chef. I ended up melting one of the cabinets and ruining my chances of ever having children.

Mother forbid me to ever touch her kitchen.

Then came the summer they diagnosed Mother with a muscular disease. Doctors told us her chances of survival were low. At first, the disease looked like poison ivy, but then she dropped forty pounds. It began attacking her heart. I stayed in her guest bedroom, helping out, preparing for the worst.

One evening, I attempted hand-cut fries with her hulking iron skillet. They came out god-awful. But she laid in her bed and ate every single one. "These are delicious," she lied. "Did you make these?"

"Yeah," I said. "But they're terrible. I don't know how you do it, Mama. I can't seem to get them right."

She set the plate down. "I don't give a blessed damn how they taste, at least you didn't buy them frozen."

"Oh, I'd never do that to you," I said.

She smiled.

Because she already knew that.

WISTFUL

She was a stunning young woman who smoked Chesterfields. She smoked them so much she paralyzed one of her vocal cords. It dropped her voice a full octave. Whenever she answered the phone, people responded by saying, "Hello, sir."

She grew up rural and believed in God. Her mother was prickly as a bag of roofing tacks, her father full-blooded Sioux. And by some stroke of fate, her daddy was born with English blue eyes. No one suspected he was Indian until a few days after he died when his squaw mother attended his funeral – in full tribal dress.

In those days, girls went to USO dances. Young women dawned their church dresses and drew ink lines up the backs of their thighs; the farm-girl version of nylon stockings. She snagged a husband at one of those dances, a captain with a toothy smile.

The petite frame that God gave her weighed in at a-buck-five, sopping wet. Her bones so small she could've passed for a Cornish hen. She was quiet, people described her as wistful – and she loved that word. If you were fortunate enough to know her, you'd learn she loved books, and plowed through them like pecans. She was also a professional portrait painter, a published poet, a fry-pan cook, an oyster fanatic, a college graduate, a Red Cross worker, and one hell of a Lutheran.

Her five children grew up to bless her as a saint. And the day my grandmother died, she tapped two fingers against her lips and mouthed, "Chesterfield." She said it only twice.

And then she met God.

ONE DAY AT WINN DIXIE

I once saw a woman smacked by her husband. It happened in the Winn Dixie parking lot when I was nineteen. I'll never forget it.

But before I continue, you ought to know something: I'm not a fighter. I'm more of an iced tea kind of guy. The altercations I've been party to, have always ended in humiliation. And this includes the kerfuffle in a youth-group van to Gatlinburg; where I may, or may not have called Javan Roberts an "ignorant bare-assed goat."

It happened like this: I saw a man and wife arguing in their front seat. He flailed his arms about and gripped her collar. She shrunk back against the window, then he drew back and hit her.

My blood turned into peanut oil.

Without knowing what to do, I dropped the groceries and jumped into my truck. I gunned through the parking lot and wheeled up on him like I was going to crunch his sedan with my tires. When our bumpers touched, I laid on my horn.

He locked eyes with me in his rearview mirror.

I flashed him a look I refer to as my *Baptist Clint Eastwood* look. The wife jumped out of the vehicle. He squealed out of the parking lot and left her behind.

The woman started crying, and explained, "He's only stressed out. Because of his job. It's not his fault."

In that moment, I wished I would've said something wise, but nineteen-year-olds, by their very nature, are not wise.

All I could answer was, "To hell with his job, and to hell with him."

Then, for no explainable reason, I took her hand.

And I said it again.

MEXICO

I expected a lot out of life when I was nine. But the truth is, I think I just wanted someone to be proud of me. Likewise, I also wanted to see Mexico, though I can't explain why.

At ten, I decided I wanted to become a sharpshooter. I practiced popping my Winchester at tin cans; I never hit anything but clouds.

At eleven and twelve, I wanted to be stick-welder, like Daddy. And at thirteen, he died. That year, I wore his oversized clothes, because they smelled like he did. Everywhere I went, I looked like a clown in baggy pants. At fourteen, the scent on his clothes faded, and I hated him for leaving us.

At sixteen, I wanted to be a sailor. After working two deckhand jobs, I decided I wanted to roam the world on a thirty-foot Hunter sailboat. And, like many ill-contrived teenage schemes, I started saving money to buy one. I stowed my dollars away in an Altoids box.

Age twenty-two: I saw Mexico by boat. It was ugly. At twenty-four, I saw Mexico again. This time from land. Still ugly. At twenty-five, I realized the world feels the same no matter where you stand, or what you stare at.

Twenty-eight: I found Daddy's wristwatch and started wearing it. Twenty-nine: I saw Mexico a third time. Ugly again. Thirty: my Altoids box wouldn't hold anymore dollars, so I bought a Hunter sailboat. At age thirty-one, I finally forgave Daddy for leaving us. At thirty-two, I decided I didn't need anyone to be proud of me.

And at age thirty-three:

I looked at my wristwatch and realized maybe I did.

TEN MILES OF TWINE

I know it's only a game. I know it's just a cork ball wrapped in yarn, covered in hide. I've taken apart my share of baseballs to see how they're made. And it's disappointing, unwrapping ten miles of twine only to find a lump of cork. I don't know what I expected to find.

A piece of candy might've been nice.

My daddy worshipped that little horsehide ball. So did his daddy, and his before him. Sometimes, the men in my family gathered outside and played ball together. They were mediocre players. They'd laugh and congratulate themselves on good throws, or how hard they hit. The more they drank, the better they played.

The better they played, the more they drank.

I can remember Uncle Lawrence standing in front of a green hay bale with a Louisville bat. My grandaddy crouched behind him, with a catcher's mitt. My father stood sixty feet away, pitching from a mound of dirt. Whenever Lawrence knocked one into the pasture, he'd say something like, "And the crowd goes wild." He'd

71

take a sip, then look at me. "Wild, I said."

Then I'd whoop and holler. I represented his unruly crowd.

Last night, I watched the second game of the World Series in my living room. On the bookshelf sits Grandaddy's mitt – which I keep oiled. Along with it: my father's mitt, a hickory bat with Grandaddy's childhood address carved in it, and a baseball my father held particularly special – though I'll never know why.

I watched the game by myself.

But not alone.

HALLOWEEN CONTESTS

Halloween night 2004: my wife, Jamie, greeted me at the door dressed like a life-sized buffalo wing. "Hey big boy," she said, shaking her darkmeat. "Are you ready to win the costume contest?" She held up a pair of electric-orange hot pants and a blonde wig.

"Contest?"

"It's a cash prize," she said. "Get dressed, you're a Hooters waitress."

"What are these, water balloons?"

The costume contest was at an honest-to-goodness honky-tonk, situated off the interstate. A handful of motorcycles parked beneath a blinking neon sign, the oversized bouncer looked an awfully lot like Rosie Greir. I showed him my ID, then tugged at the seat of my orange knicker shorts.

I didn't care for the way Rosie winked at me.

The establishment was ablaze with costumed folks. And when contestants took the stage, the crowd went berserk. A man dressed like Jaws ate red Jell-O using only his fins. Next: an inebriated Kermit the Frog impersonator. After that, a fire swallower.

Then it was our turn.

Jamie swatted my rear. "Make me proud, Tiffany."

Together, we took the stage. Jamie cued the DJ and "Proud Mary" blasted through the speakers. I stood paralyzed beneath the lights like a slug. Then, something happened, the pulsating music worked its way down into my tailfeathers.

And I let myself go.

There, before three hundred of my peers, I flipped my blonde wig and shimmied my hindparts like co-captain of the Auburn University cheer squad. And when Jamie poured hot-wing sauce all over my spurious bosoms, someone in the audience stood and hollered, "I see London, I see France!"

I wiped my eyes and glanced across the stage to see a pair of uninhabited neon-orange Daisy Dukes.

We won.

FRONT PORCHES

As a chubby kid, my mother took great pleasure in Halloween. She went to elaborate lengths to manufacture clever ensembles that capitalized on my circular figure.

One Halloween, she swaddled me in eight rolls of Ace bandages. When I visited Mrs. Louise's front porch the woman remarked, "Oh, how cute. Are you the Michelin Man?"

"No ma'am, I'm a mummy."

"Oh Harold, come quick. Look at the fat little mummy."

Harold asked if I could cut any deals on fifteen-inch LTX Michelin Defenders. The answer was no. So, I tap danced a version of the Charleston. Harold dug into his pockets, he gave me two dimes, and a ball of lint.

Another year: Mother dressed me in a newspaper-stuffed burlap sack. I was an honest-to-goodness Yukon Gold potato. When I showed up on doorsteps, I'd rattle my empty jack-o-lantern and say, "Donate to save endangered French fries."

"Come quick, Harold, it's a fat little rock."

"Does he dance?" Harold asked.

And then I'd do the jitterbug until I was out of breath. Harold handed me a waded up dry cleaning receipt, tweezers, and a breath mint.

The following Halloween, Mother dressed me as a baker, in all white. I wore a tall hat and carried a rolling pin.

"Oh Harold, it's a fat little chef."

"Actually," I said. "I'm a baker."

Harold came to the door. "He looks like the Pilsbury Doughboy. Does he do the high-pitched laugh?"

Mrs. Louise swatted her husband. "Don't be cruel."

Harold set his beer down and pulled a fifty-dollar bill out of his wallet. We locked eyes. Tentatively, Harold pressed his finger against my bellybutton, just to see what might happen.

Well.

I walked away with fifty dollars. That's what happened.

UNCLE FRANK

At eighteen, I helped my great uncle, Frank, clean out his attic. Not because I wanted to, but because I liked him. I enjoyed the way he talked. Everything Frank said sounded like he was moderately pissed off.

They stationed my Uncle Frank on the U.S.S. Uruguay, in North Africa, during the second World War. He bore a crude green tattoo on his burly forearm to prove it.

"We were a transport ship," he told me. "We moved supplies from here to there. I was a glorified lower back."

My uncle, who joined the Navy to fight the Japanese and impress girls, lifted crates, swept floors, and smoked cigarettes. There wasn't much glory in it.

"Our lieutenant-commander was a real sumbitch. All he did was bark orders. He was tall, with a hard face. He always walked like he had somewhere to be. Not like you and I walk."

"But one night, our lieutenant-commander broke all the rules, and he fraternized with us men. We saw him at the local bar, he'd been there a while, he was already liquored up. Well, one thing led to another, he started arm wrestling with us boys."

Uncle Frank flexed his bicep like he was a young lion – with three herniated discs, and a high blood pressure. "When it was my turn at bat, the Lieutenant Commander was already drunk and worn out. I beat him. Twice. He bought me drinks the rest of the night."

My uncle lowered his voice. "And that's the story of how I beat Lieutenant Commander Bryant in arm wrestling." Frank paused for effect. "But most people knew him as Bear Bryant."

JUGS OF MILK

Yesterday, I watched a woman feed feral cats behind the supermarket. She poured a jug of milk into a pan; they swarmed her in hopes of affection. The woman squatted down to pet each of them, and they all waited their turn.

The day before, I saw a boy fall off his bike in the parking lot. An elderly man saw it, too. He ran to the boy, and helped him off the ground, like a grandfather might do. The two of them complete strangers.

Earlier that same morning, a black Nissan Altima stopped on the highway, blocking a mile of traffic behind it. A man leapt out of the driver's side wearing a nice suit. He scurried into the center of the road, picked up a turtle, and set it on the shoulder.

Last week, in Jacksonville, Florida: I saw a gentleman sitting on a park bench. He had a wiry beard, and a shopping buggy filled with the entirety of his earthly belongings. I counted at least six people who donated money or food. One woman even gave him a blanket.

Only yesterday evening, a young girl locked herself out of her car. Three of us onlookers managed to jimmy her door open without harming the vehicle. One lucky young man even got her phone number. He got so excited, he forgot how to pronounce his own name.

I know lot of people don't think there's much good out there in the world. God knows, they have every right to think that way.

But I know some feral cats who believe otherwise.

TO MY UNBORN CHILD

To the child I've never had, and probably never will:

If you were a girl, I'd pray you weren't too beautiful, but plain and average-looking, like your daddy. There are too many good-looking people in the world as it is. To hell with perfect faces; be the prettiest soul. And if you were a boy, I'd want you to be chubby, and slow on the baseball field. Being mediocre is more fun than being the best.

No matter who you are, I want you to climb trees, and garner lots of scrapes. They'll decorate your skin with memories that become good stories with age.

Try to learn the difference between good and bad biscuits. Eat fried gizzards, livers, and gristle whenever possible. Everyone reaches for the drumsticks first; they're missing out. And I want you to eat too much ice cream. Life's too short not to eat ice cream. Learn as many jokes as you can, from start to finish. Never, ever rush the punchline.

And, I wish you didn't have to watch someone you love die. It feels like losing your face, your stomach, and your mind all at once. But one day you will, and it will make you fully human. It's part of this mysterious suffrage we call life.

Love someone I'd never choose for you. Make choices that might embarrass me. Don't pay attention to anyone's advice unless you want to. Not even mine. Because the truth is, darling, I'm no different than you are. I don't know a damn thing about life. And I don't know much about love.

All I know is that it's harder for folks who know they're good-looking.

BARN OWLS

The evening I found my mother on the back porch, sitting still, it worried me. That woman never sat still, not even if her life depended on it.

"It's Chuck," she said. "He's broken it off with me. He's found someone else."

The next thing I knew, I was driving down a dark gravel road with the windows down. I'd left in a hurry, I didn't even have socks on. When I reached Chuck's place, I revved my engine, kicking up dirt in his driveway. I clenched my fists and stomped onto his porch. An abundance of testosterone in a boy's bloodstream will make him do such things.

Chuck came to the door and saw me breathing heavy. "Hey buddy, what's the matter?"

I wanted to shout something ugly, say something about my mother's honor. I wanted to smear Chuck on the pavement for breaking her heart. More than that, I wanted my father back; I wanted to walk into the woods and disappear like a barn owl.

"H-H-How could you?" was all I could mutter before

crying.

Chuck took me into his arms. He brought me inside, made coffee, and out the kindness of his heart, explained himself to a cotton-picking eighteen-year-old. Then, Chuck did something odd; he taught me to play chess. I was terrible at it. We played five hours until I fell asleep on his sofa.

When I went to leave the next morning, I found a chess set in the front seat of my truck. A note read, "Cheer up, you'll forget all about me one day, partner."

He was wrong.

You never forget how to play chess.

WORRY

My grandfather said once, "If there's one thing I wish I could save you from it'd be worry." Then he'd touch my shoulder and say, "Whenever you start to worry, I want you to say to yourself, 'I'm a rich man, and God gives a damn about me.'" Then, he'd puff that pipe of his and laugh quietly to himself.

Worry? I don't think I started until age nine. I worried about trivial things; that Mother's fried chicken would be lukewarm if I was tardy for dinner.

At sixteen, I worried hangovers wouldn't dissipate until old age. Almost like God's way of saying, "Beer before liquor, and I will smite thy wicked little hindparts."

When I hit my mid-twenties, I worried Jamie and I couldn't make babies. The doctor conducted a series of tests that I'm ashamed to even tell you about. In the end, he said our plumbing worked fine. "You need to calm down, son," he said. "Stress and worry will destroy you."

I explained to him that I was Baptist.

He wrote me a script for horse tranquilizers.

The truth is, I know fear is destructive. I still worry about the price of gas, the World Series, that my sniffle is really black plague, that I don't drink enough water, that I eat too much fried shrimp, that I don't tell people how much I love them. I worry mankind is going to blow himself up one day. I worry my cornbread is going to burn if I get the skillet too hot.

But, then again.

I'm a very a rich man, and God gives a damn about me.

LIVING FOREVER

Gluten kills. I read that in a magazine. The article went on to explain bread would kill me if I so much as glanced at it in the supermarket. The nightly news, however, told me the opposite, stating white bread prolongs life. On the broadcast, they featured a one-hundred-twenty-year-old Frenchman tearing up a baguette the size of a life raft.

That same week, NBC claimed alcohol, even in low doses – say, two beers – would age me so fast I'd piss my pants and slip into a coma before the broadcast ended.

The next morning, my wife said the newspaper reported red wine is the fountain of youth. Meet Giuseppe, a four-hundred-year-old Sicilian who plows through two bottles of Merlot each night. Sure, Giuseppe has nine ex-wives and can't go to the bathroom without an ordained priest, but he's alive.

What about Chinese elders who've been alive since the invention of underpants? Reputedly, all they consume is poultry and gallons of tea. That's the big secret? I hate to break it to you, Southerners have been eating that way forever. Take my uncle: he drinks buckets of sweet tea and eats fried chicken every night of the week. His blood pressure is high enough to power a nail gun.

I suppose I don't know why everyone's trying to live so long anyway. What's wrong with being dead? I was dead millions of years before I was alive, I didn't even feel it. Perhaps my ninety-one-year-old uncle had a point. "You wanna know how to live forever?" He cracked open a Budweiser. "Love someone. That's how."

Well, that's utterly ridiculous. But then, what would he know?

He still eats gluten.

HER

My first memory of her is in the hospital, she was a newborn. She smelled funny and made the same grunting noises bullfrogs make before you gig them. The nurse told me she was making a stinky in her diaper. I'd never heard it called a "stinky" before. I rather liked that particular turn of phrase.

She wasn't yet five when Daddy died, she doesn't remember him. So, she has no idea how much she resembles him; her gait, her toothy grin, her self-effacing humor.

When she got older, she and I delivered the morning paper together. It was the worst job I ever had. We woke at three every morning and threw four hundred newspapers to the western side of the city. Then, we'd watch the sun climb over the Gulf of Mexico, she'd fall asleep in the passenger seat.

The truth is, I'm the closest to a father she's ever known, unlucky for her, because I was only a boy when Daddy died. I didn't know how to be parental, much less braid a five-year-old's hair.

But sometimes, boys turn into adults too damn fast.

It's unfair. Thirteen-year-olds aren't supposed to be so serious. They're not supposed to do the laundry, kiss boo-boos, or talk like grown-ups.

Well.

Perhaps one day, she and I will get to try it again, in the next world. Maybe up there, second childhoods are handed out at the front door. Maybe I'll be different. Maybe we'll laugh more and cry less. I guess what I'm trying to say is, I love you, Sarah.

God help me.

You're going to have a baby.

OH TO BE FREE

If you ever visit Laurel Hill, Florida with your wife and dog, don't open the truck door, one of them will run off. If you're unlucky, both will.

It might happen like this:

You might be at a gas station. Perhaps, your dog catches sight of a squirrel, or develops restless leg syndrome. Your dog might bound out of the cab faster than a spit stain. Well, that's what mine did. Immediately trailing behind her was my uncoordinated wife. The two of them bounded across an open field like kids chasing an ice cream truck.

We tracked Ellie up to Florala, Alabama, where I taunted her with a Slim Jim. "Here Ellie, c'mon. Daddy's not mad. Looky, Daddy's happy. You're so pretty, yes you are."

Ellie made eye-contact, licked her who-who, then trotted off toward Canada.

When I got back to the truck, my wife had taken over at the wheel. "Get in!" Jamie barked.

She sped through ten miles of dirt before I could even

shut my passenger door. "Hang on!" she yelled. "I see her!"

We finally found Ellie Mae sniffing daisies on a dead-end gravel road. Jamie slammed the brakes, then clicked on the hazard lights in a kind of Mexican standoff. But Ellie Mae didn't even notice the crazy brunette with the twitching eyelid. Ellie meandered into a ditch and wallowed in the muddy water like a baby sow on Labor Day.

Jamie rolled up her pant legs and said, "I'm going to get that little bitch."

It sounded simple enough.

Except, ditches in Alabama can be twelve-feet deep.

THE OLDER BOYS

When I was twelve, I caught two older kids picking on a boy we called Slim, who was very different than the rest of us. They slammed Slim's fingers in a barn door because he talked with a lisp. Ruined his hand.

I once knew a girl raped by her stepfather. The man skipped town before anyone ever found out. No one could prove it happened, and no one believed the girl. He's still out there doing god-knows-what. The girl, in and out of drug rehab.

Ten years ago, I watched a man with Tennessee tags run over a golden retriever on Highway 98. He kept driving eighty miles per hour like it never happened. That little dog's collar-tag read, "Buck." I'll never forget that animal.

A black seventeen-year-old was found on a playground, in North Carolina, hung from a swing set, dangling by a rope. He was the cousin of my friend. It was an old-fashioned lynching. His killers, likely college sophomores, chasing skirts, screaming at football games until they're hoarse.

Every two minutes someone is raped in America. Each day, one hundred five are so depressed they commit suicide; thirty-three hundred die in car accidents; fifteen hundred die of cancer; three hundred are shot. Anyone who calls oneself a human-being has a right to declare this world bound for Hell in a knitting basket.

How a thirty-two-year-old man, who talks with a lisp and has a messed up hand, has the gall to believe in love, is beyond my understanding.

But somehow, he does.

And Slim believes love will win.

ANIMATED

Of all the places in all the world, we first met in a bookstore. She asked me where the bathrooms were, saying, "Jeezus, I've gotta pee like a racehorse."

The first thing you should know about her is that she's an animated speaker who uses her hands when she talks. And everything she says is tinted with a hint of pissiness, like she's close to losing her already short temper.

During our first chance meeting, we talked about life, trivial things. We talked about fashion, good versus evil; and George Jones versus the idiocy that passes for modern-day country music.

The first thing I noticed was her affliction for telling the truth. It's a curse. And that isn't to say she doesn't care what you think about her. She most certainly does. It's just that God didn't give her the ability to blow much smoke. This problem is only made worse when she pours a few drinks down her gullet.

You'll just have to take my word for that.

She looks awkward in dresses, most tom-girls do.

Without her glasses on she looks like a raccoon missing his mask. Her hair is flawless, so is her Creek Indian skin. Her ears are big like her daddy's. Her eyes look sad even when they're happy, just like his did. She owns an unerring set of tastebuds; the woman would rather die than eat food that isn't worth dying for. She's tall, she can lift a metric ton, and she bruises easily — both inside and out. When she cries it feels like the whole world turns black and gray, swallowing up the sun.

It's not every day you meet someone you love in a bookstore.

A HUNDRED DOLLARS

I lost my pocket knife. It happened years ago, and it nearly killed me. I can't think of anything more sacred than a pocket knife, to a boy. I own several. I have one that looks like it could skin a Kodiak bear, I use it for opening bills. Another knife accompanied me to the Grand Canyon, I couldn't have survived without it. I used it to carve walking sticks, open beer bottles, and slice through Twinkie wrappers.

But the knife I lost, disappeared when I totaled my truck. That is to say, the first truck I totaled – not to be confused with the other two I've sent to the be with Jesus.

Immediately after the wreck, the paramedic told me to gather my things. He told me to make it "snappy," then he called me "speedy," a name I didn't particularly care for. And I forgot the knife in my glovebox.

God knows whatever happened to it.

I first got that knife when I was twelve. I sat before our Christmas tree with only two gifts bearing my name. The first, a pair of slacks from Mother. I did my best to

97

smile. But the truth was, the last thing anyone wants on the morning of Christ's birth is something that needs regular ironing.

The next gift was a tiny box. A nice pocket knife that must've cost Daddy nearly a hundred dollars. My initials were inscribed on the blade, and it took my breath away. Well, I think about that knife a lot. I hope someone has it. And if somebody does, I hope he gives it to his boy.

Because.

All boys need a good pocket knife.

ALL MY THANKS

I suppose, I'd like to say thank you to my sixth-grade teacher, Mrs. Doerkson. Without her, I wouldn't be writing. In fact, you wouldn't even be reading this right now.

Then, I'd like to thank my older cousin, Lora, for handing me a cigarette when I was thirteen, saying, "Here, take a big drag off this." That was the last time I ever smoked another cigarette. Likewise, damn you, Andrew, for attempting the same thing with chewing tobacco.

Thank you Goldie, my childhood golden retriever, she taught me unconditional love. To my boyhood-girlfriend Katie, the only girl I've ever known to share my allergic reaction to poison ivy. And to her mother, for introducing me to oatmeal baths.

Thank you to John Wayne, for teaching me how to hold a straight face, and to my babysitter Charlotte for introducing me to John Wayne. To Billy-Jay, Skip, and Robert, who taught me how to shoot quail. And to Cody, my chocolate Labrador, who never retrieved a single quail.

I'm grateful to my mother, who suffered through my adolescence. She bought my first typewriter and has read every story I've ever written. For learning how to grieve with me. I'll die with her name on my heart.

Thank you Lyle, for the World Series blowout; the chicken wings, calamari, steamed mussels, and fried cheese balls. Thank you to his wife, Sherry, who has non-verbally demonstrated how to be oneself, without apologizing for it.

Thank you to my wife, Jamie, for growing up with me.

And thank you Mrs. Doerkson, for once saying, "Anyone can say 'thanks,' but a grateful boy uses a pen to do it."

And thank you.

For reading this.

ABOUT ROBERT

The first thing you ought to know about Robert was that he never looked you in the eye when he spoke. It was too much. Daddy said it was because Robert had been to prison as a young man.

Robert had pure white hair, old skin, and he smoked like a chimney. Often, he'd show up to our farm early for work, with a gift for me. Once, he gave me a notepad. Every page had a handwritten scripture coinciding with a calendar date.

"Used to read this every day," Robert said. "Brought me a lot of good." He tapped his forehead. "Got it memorized now."

"You memorized all this?"

He nodded. "Go ahead. Test me."

I flipped to a page. "April seventh?"

Robert stared at the sky, concentrating. "Naked I came from my mother's womb, and naked I shall return thither. The Lord gave, and the Lord hath taken away."

I turned to another. "February second."

"Greater is He that is in thee, than he that is in the

101

world."

Then, I thumbed to my birth date.

Robert closed his eyes. "Have I not commanded thee, be strong and of good courage; and neither be thou dismayed; for the Lord thy God is with thee whithersoever thou goest."

I wrinkled up my face. "Huh?"

"It means you don't have to be afraid."

"I guess it's my verse, it falls on my birthday."

Robert rolled up his sleeve to show a wrinkled forearm. Crude purplish ink words ran lengthwise along his arm. "I can guaran-damn-tee you, the verse is true, son."

Well, he ought to have known.

Because it was Robert's verse too.

PONY RIDES

"Little Jamie had her daddy wrapped around her finger," said Jamie's mother. "Would you believe, one year for her birthday she asked him for an honest-to-goodness pony?"

Jamie interjected, "I did not..." She cleared her throat. "... all I said was that I wouldn't mind if Daddy happened to buy one."

Her mother continued. "Well, it's no surprise, for Jamie's eighth birthday, he bought her a god-forsaken miniature horse. She'd crawl upon that horrid beast and ride in circles until her hindparts fell asleep."

Jamie smiled, recalling the pleasant tingling of pins and needles in her plump saddle-sore cheeks.

"Oh," her mother said. "You should've seen Jamie. She had a little cowboy hat, boots, and a cap gun strung around her waist like Dale Evans. She'd fire her gun in the air shouting, 'Mama, look, look! I'm King Bear Bryant!'"

"King Bear Bryant?" I interrupted. "He didn't ride horses."

Jamie shot me in the groin with her imaginary pistol. "No one asked you."

"The point is," said her mother. "Jamie could've asked her daddy to buy all Birmingham, Alabama and he would've made an offer. So, I finally got smart about things."

"What do you mean?"

"Well, I successfully convinced little Jamie we needed a new car for her ninth birthday. A nice one, green, with tan leather seats. Because real cowgirls deserve leather seats."

"You're joking."

"Nope. I got a little horsepower of my own that year," she said, slapping her imaginary stallion on its tail-end. "Who's King Bear Bryant now, kid?"

You are, Miss Mary.

You are.

GROWING PAINS

At fifteen, my legs grew so fast my tendons couldn't keep up. I'd moan as though someone had stretched me like Silly Putty. The growth spurts made me walk funny; imagine if you will, Charlie Chaplin in need of fiber supplementation.

For two months, I hobbled with a cane. The doctor assured me I'd survive, then he asked which flavor of lollipop I wanted. I informed him that fifteen-year-olds didn't eat suckers.

So, he gave me a cigar and a shot of bourbon.

It was during this period of life I developed a thick layer of body-fur, common to species of timber wolf phylum. Almost overnight, I sprouted hair on my chest, face, and back. One of the girls swimming down by the creek took me aside one day. "Look," she said. "There's something you should know. Your body-hair, it's gross. You should shave that." And the other girls giggled.

I went home and shaved every damn hair from my body with a straight-razor, even the hair growing on the tops of my ears. Then, I looked at myself in the mirror,

Band-Aids covering nicks on my chest, and I sobbed.

Mother found me. "What's wrong?"

"I'm ugly. Just look at me."

She wrapped her arms around me. "Oh, I'm glad you feel this way, honey."

"You are?"

"Yes, it's a blessing that things are so painful for you right now. The truth is, I'm happy for it."

"Why would you say such a thing?"

"Because, as adults we're supposed to be kindhearted and compassionate toward others. Encouraging to our neighbors."

"Yeah. So?"

She touched my bandage. "People who've never felt pain have a hard time doing that."

MY BELIEFS

None of my beliefs are mine. I didn't come up with any of them. The same probably goes for you.

Take for instance: my ideas about happiness. My grandfather said the secret to being happy was not to worry about being happy.

His advice is a lot harder than it sounds.

My grandmother assumed a different approach. She said that to be happy, I should think like an eighty-year-old. "Elderly folks are too old to bother with youthful urges, or fantasies of success. All they care about is family, friends, and getting enough fiber."

So, I invested in velcro tennis shoes and a jar of Metamucil.

My ideals on alcohol come from Grandmother too. "A man is always entitled to beer or bourbon; if he wants anything more, he'd better make sure he owns a Bible."

My great uncle Lawrence, on professionalism: "People who promote themselves annoy the damn spit out of everyone else. Nobody's half as good as they say.

Let your work will speak for itself and shut your mouth."

About friendship, from Uncle Sam: "If you can't run with folks better than you, run alone."

About food, from my wife, Jamie: "If I don't eat something quick, I'm about to cuss someone the hell out. Hey you. Yeah you. What're you looking at, pisswad?"

My views on etiquette from Aunt Eulah: "If you don't have good manners, you'd better have fast reflexes."

And, my views about love, from Daddy: "Everything dies, Sean. Even me. So, I want you to do something. Find someone to love, because that's about as close as you'll get to living forever. You hear me?"

Yes, Daddy.

Yes I do.

CLEAN EATERS

Yesterday, a man in the checkout line glanced at my box of Jiffy cornbread mix, "That junk will kill you some day." He handed me a business card. On the card was a picture of himself, bench pressing a herculean tractor tire. The man said, "Call me if you ever decide to start eating clean."

Eat clean?

I learned about this as a boy. Once, I came to supper wearing soiled, grass-stained jeans. Mother took one look and said, "If you're going to eat at this table, take a shower. Because in this house, we eat clean, dammit."

The truth is, I've heard of these anti-cornbread regimes before. I have a friend who follows the "Caveman Diet." Nothing touches his lips unless it's something an ancient man with severe constipation might've eaten.

Once at a dinner party, I offered him a beer. He laughed, then went outside and lapped water from a mud puddle. "Cavemen don't drink beer," he said.

"How about some cornbread?"

He scoffed. "No thanks, my wife brought kale chips and a leftover goat femur."

While I admit, cavemen didn't eat cornbread, they only lived to the ripe-old-ages of sophomores. And, I'll take a wild guess: I'm almost certain they didn't bench press tractor tires very often.

My friend explained, "Our sledge-hammers and tractor tires are only symbols of power."

Well sir, thirty miles outside town, tractor tires aren't symbols. They're muddy. The men that use them have beer bellies and high cholesterol. The same men who grow soybeans; the same soybeans that go into fourteen-dollar caveman protein bars.

Which no self-respecting caveman would ever eat.

Unless he ran out of cornbread and beer.

NURSES

I was in love with my mother's friend, Vivian. Mother said she was the most dedicated nursing student God ever created. But she was more than that.

She was perfect.

Whenever Vivian was around, I was unable to speak in complete sentences. It might've been her long dark hair, or her almond eyes, which both seemed to say, "Run away with me, damn you." And I wasn't discouraged that Vivian was twenty years my senior. After all, in some third-world cultures, adolescent romances were considered modern. Trendy, even.

One year, when Vivian's semester-final exams were nearing, she approached me with a proposition.

"Sean," she said. "I know you paint and draw."

I felt my face turn the color of a Venus Eagle cherry.

Vivian explained, "My professor's agreed to let my class use notes on the final test. But there's a catch. My notes have to fit onto this." She held an index card. "Can you write small enough to do it?"

"Golly, your skin looks soft."

"I'd pay you for your trouble."

"The softest I've ever seen, and I'll bet you smell like flowers."

"Are you even listening?"

"A whole mountainside of flowers."

Well, that night I stayed up thirteen hours writing with the tiniest penmanship conceivable, using a magnifying glass. When I completed the notecard, hardly any white was showing. On the bottom of the card, I wrote a singular sentence in the form of a question. Which would remain unanswered until the day of Vivian's graduation; when she proclaimed from the podium, "No, I won't marry you, Sean!"

The auditorium erupted in laughter.

Then that ugly hussy blew me a kiss.

IT IS NOT FAIR

I'm sorry your car is junk, that you have to air up your tires to take it anywhere. I'm sorry your mattress is flat, that your back hurts. I hate that you can't fall asleep because of a dull pain that won't quit. No one should have to feel pain.

I'm sorry someone hurt you. That some idiot lied and made you feel less than beautiful. It's not right. And dammit, I hate that you feel like no one pays attention to you anymore. I'm certain there's a perfect life you've imagined for yourself, and this isn't it. Not by a long shot. I know you want to show the world – especially your enemies – how high you can fly.

But you're not there, and you might never be.

I don't know why we're not allowed to have, feel, see, touch, or hold the things we want; let alone the things we need.

There doesn't seem to be a reason why some suffer, and others sip fruity drinks. Why some have disease, and others have baby showers. I don't know why a mother of four dies at twenty-five, or a healthy man shoots innocent people.

But I'm sorry the doctor gave you bad news. I'm sorry your dog passed. Christ, I'm sorry your daddy died. Whoever you are, if I could rid you of it, I would.

All I can say is: I believe something is at work, even though I don't know what the hell it is. I just know that it doesn't matter what kind of mess you're in.

Because it's going to be okay.

NUMBERS

"Always look out for three," my grandfather would say in an almost cryptic way. "You hear me, son? You'll find threes are everywhere in life, look for them." Then he'd laugh, relight his pipe, and refuse to explain himself. I'd tried to decipher what in the world such a phrase meant, but I had no earthly idea.

Still, I did what he said. I paid attention to the number three wherever I looked. And I don't know if you've noticed, but if you keep your good eye out, you'll see threes everywhere. In football, basketball, and baseball. In pastrami sandwiches, electrical outlets, or on your TV remote.

The number three is in stories: beginnings, middles, and ends. Smeared all over religion: God, Jesus, and Billy Graham. In the Bible. Or in Baptist picnics: Bud, Miller, and Ultra.

But my grandfather wasn't talking about those things. And I learned that on the day of his funeral.

An elderly gentleman came up to me with his hat in his hands. "Your grandfather was a good man," he said.

"We were friends. We used to have long conversations, late into the night, back during the war. He was my captain at the time, a lot older than me. Took me under his wing, saved a young dope like me from sudden death on two separate occasions."

The man wiped something from his eye. "Your grandaddy was not the kind of fella who just looked out for number one." Then, the man shook my hand.

His name was Ronald.

But most folks call him, Three.

FIREPLACES

All I want for Thanksgiving," said Jamie. "Is a fireplace."

So, Thanksgiving 2006, we selected a cabin perched in the Virginian Mountains. The rental advertised spectacular views, and a grandiose fireplace.

We left town the morning before Thanksgiving. Our truck packed so tight a gnat couldn't squeeze inside without first going on a diet.

Our highway trip got off to a good start. After six hours, Jamie and I were singing with the Oakridge Boys on the radio. I held the Coke-bottle microphone doing my best William Lee Golden.

All of a sudden, a loud crash interrupted us. I checked the mirror and saw a red cooler skipping across the highway behind me. Followed by our suitcases, charcoal grill, somersaulting microwave, and finally my tailgate itself.

After pulling over, I was only able to salvage one frozen suitcase from the ditch.

When I climbed back into the cab, the domelights

were dim and the heater wasn't blowing. "Jamie, why is the truck off?"

She shrugged. "I thought you shut it off."

I turned the key. Nothing. Turned the key again. Jack squat.

Two hours later, after a jumpstart from a Clayton County deputy, we hit the road again. By three in the morning, we limped into Powdersville, South Carolina, where my alternator went on to Glory.

I pulled into the first stop off Highway 85. The Pink Flamingo Motor Inn; free HBO and green floral carpet. For an extra twenty dollars, they let us upgrade to the honeymoon suite – which had a brick fireplace.

By all accounts, it should've been the worst damn Thanksgiving ever. And if might've been.

If not for that fireplace.

OPEN HOUSES

Thanksgiving represented the time of year my mother opened our home to strangers. It was when Mister Charlie carried a van-load of visitors to our place, those who couldn't afford turkeys. People down on their luck, with kids. Working-class folks, humble enough to drop their names into a wooden box at the Methodist church, asking for holiday help.

Mister Charlie threw the van door open, out jumped a mess of kids. They darted across eighty sprawling acres of alfalfa and fescue like freed prisoners. They played with our goats, teased the chickens, climbed trees, and swung on my tire swing.

Mother and four other ladies cooked like Hebrew slaves, preparing the biggest spread you ever saw. And when it was suppertime, Mister Charlie hobbled to the door and called us in with an honest-to-goodness trumpet.

I was a glutton. One year, I ate so much I vomited in the pasture. There were simply too many casseroles to sample.

At the end of the evening, one of the men sitting in our den asked Mother why she opened her home on Thanksgiving.

"Well," Mother said, topping off his strawberry wine. "I don't do it for you."

Mister Charlie interjected, "She does it for the Lord."

"No, I don't," Mother said. "My husband's dead, and it's lonely out here. Sometimes, the kids and I go days without saying two words. And well, I don't want to be alone on Thanksgiving."

"Dammit," Mister Charlie said, raising his glass. "No one can fault you for that, honey." Everyone joined in raising glasses because they knew very well what loneliness was.

And how nice it was not to feel it.

THE ART OF CLIMBING

Climbing trees is an art, not a skill. I've known fellas who could scale trees better than house-cats.

Take, for instance, Dee: that boy could climb using only his arms, no feet. It was stupefying. Me? I couldn't do a single chin-up. Boys like me, with chubby legs, were built for helping their grandmothers bake cookies.

Dee, spider-monkeyed to the top, then screamed to me, "Bet you can't come and get me, titty-baby!"

To which Titty-Baby responded, "I'm coming up there to wipe your ass with a boot."

I got a running start and leapt into the tree. Soon, I was frighteningly high up. When I made it to Dee, he said, "Good luck getting down, cookie-boy." Then he disappeared down the tree.

You see, no one explained disembarking a tree was fifty times harder than climbing it. But, this is especially true for boys with fat little faces. So, I sat straddling a limb until the sun went down.

My father's voice startled me. "What're you doing up there?" Without awaiting my response, he climbed the tree like an acrobat, flinging skinny legs over limbs. He made Dee look like a joke.

"How're you so good at climbing?" I asked.

"I'm an ironworker," he said. "I climb things for a living. When I was your age, I was overweight. I couldn't climb worth a damn."

"How'd you learn?"

He sat next to me and looked at the stars. "Oh, I suppose I grew up, and I had to climb big things, like all adults do. Without anybody's help. Somehow, I learned. And you will too."

Well.

He wasn't talking about trees.

And neither am I.

WHAT HAPPENED TO ALUMINUM PERCOLATORS?

I wonder where the world will be in fifty years? We're already different than we were a decade ago. Folks have replaced tin coffee cans with plastic ones. It feels like something alien. Plastic coffee cans; as I live and breathe. Now what am I going to store roofing nails in?

How about aluminum percolators, or sink drainboards, hand-cranked meat grinders, washtubs, cast iron waffle-makers, or enameled Dutch ovens? These things are relics now. Gone. Maybe forever. Well, I feel sorry for the child who's only tasted chicken and dumplings from a Teflon-coated electric crockpot. Dumplings are not supposed to be made in crockpots.

Towns have changed, too. The town my grandmother grew up in, once a little speck on the map, now has a supermarket with a salad bar and live lobsters.

My grandmother and her friends used to ride out to the edge of town to drink corn liquor in a tall barn, one that doubled as a dance hall. There, the men who played guitars and fiddles weren't musicians. They were farmers' sons, mill workers, responsible men. Back then, I understand that young ladies were accomplished cooks, bakers, launderers, who knew how to iron table linens. If you would've asked my grandmother, she would've told you, "By fifteen, we were full-fledged adults."

Furthermore, kids today don't even know what corn liquor is. They drink craft beer that costs more than a new pair of pants.

Houses were different, then. My cousin, the architect, calls my grandmother's farmhouse an architectural wonder. "Look at this floor plan," he said once. "They built things different than we build today. Back then they used lots of doors and windows, and adjoined rooms, to keep air flowing because there was no air conditioning." My cousin demonstrated by opening every door and window. A stiff breeze filled the upper level of the home.

Today, my grandmother's house has a big wooden pole out front that supplies the homestead with electricity, phone service, digital cable, and wireless internet. Internet. My grandaddy would pass a kidney stone, then flop like a fish in his grave if he saw that.

Long ago, Grandaddy claimed regular people talked less.

"Talked less?" I asked.

"Yep, we didn't have phones. In my childhood, the closest phone was three houses down the road. The only times we spoke was when we saw each other in town. Well nowadays, young folks talk five times as much as we did. You use the phone first thing in the morning. And now they have those newfangled cellular carphones.

Those things are going to change the world, you mark my words. It'll be a wonder your voices don't give out before you turn fifty. All you do is chit chat."

Silence isn't the only thing disappearing. The horse-drawn farm implements my great-great-grandfather have vanished altogether. They are rusted pieces of metal now. My great-uncle told me a local restaurant corporation offered to buy the implements for landscape decor. And so, the plow my grandfather guided, while yelling, "Gee," or "Haw," now sits in front of a Cracker Barrel, for snot-nosed kids to play on.

It's not that I don't like modernized advancements, I do. I don't know where I'd be without Apple Computer products, or my memory foam pillow. But it's not all for the better. Take for instance: the last time I went to a baseball game, the entirety of people below the age of forty-five stared at iPhones instead of at the field. They took more selfies than they did cheer for base hits. Which as it turned out, didn't matter. We lost horribly.

Handheld devices are more plentiful than horse apples. And lots of people read on them. Whole books and magazines. So much so, the traditional paperback-book industry is rumored to go belly up within the next hundred years. Belly up.

Also newspapers. Newspapers have the lowest readership they've ever had. Experts are already calling newspapers a thing of the past.

There was a time when most of the free world read a printed paper newspaper with their eggs and bacon. They got ink on their hands, and it was the kind that could kill you if you licked it. So said my grandmother. Today, only a little over twenty percent read a paper newspaper. They've also traded in bacon and eggs, for scrambled tofu and coconut milk. Gag me.

You want more? Only three percent of America smokes a pipe anymore. Two percent are farmers. And only one percent play the accordion.

Which means I have no peers.

Today, more people own microwaves than ever before in history. Folks cook rice in plastic packets. They buy catfish that was bred in China. For firewood, they use logs made from recycled newspaper; only a few bucks at Kroger. Then, they pay four dollars for a cup of hand-brewed coffee down the street, while refusing to sit at a table inside since there is no Wi-Fi.

Today, fewer young women grow flowers in their front yard than ever – especially compared to fifty years ago. And even though there are a few knitters out there, a survey found that hardly any young girls make things with yarn, even fewer quilt. Another study asked girls how often they wore dresses. Over half the answers were, "less than three times per year."

Three times. Christmas, Easter, and an occasional small-claims court appearance.

Boys don't fist fight like they used to, which I suppose is a good thing. Over sixty percent of boys in America claim they've never even been in a fight at all.

At *all*.

Well, not me. It seems like every Saturday I had a bloody lip, and my mother didn't think a thing about it.

One teacher says, "We've done boys a disservice. Boys aren't allowed to be rough anymore, their animosity builds until they do horrible, cruel things to each other. That's why I think we're seeing more bullying than ever before. We don't let boys settle things. We try to do it for them."

"But isn't it wrong to fight?" I asked.

"Sure. But it's not unforgivable, is it?"

Is this a trick question?

She went on, "Why, if a boy raised his fists on the playground today, he'd be expelled from the school system, and sent to Alcatraz. Don't you think that's a little harsh?"

Silly woman. Alcatraz closed down decades ago.

Still, she's right. It's difficult to be a true boy today. Tackle football is under review by state legislatures, and has been speculated to be a sport off-limits to boys under college age in the future. Even in Little League baseball, folks are petitioning to using softer balls and ban wooden bats altogether. I don't take a stance on these issues, because I don't have kids. But I *do* like wooden bats.

I won't touch the subject of guns, except to say: my grandfather taught me how to shoot quail with an 1879 Sharps rifle. And I count it as one of the most special memories of my entire existence. Like my grandfather once said, "There's no better flavor than food you killed yourself." He was right. If I wouldn't have learned to hunt, I might not care for quail, squirrel, or wild turkey doused in brown gravy.

Gravy.

God, I hope we don't forget about gravy. I hope we don't forget about Dutch ovens, or wooden bats. I half-wish our cellphones would quit working. Not forever, just for a little while. Just long enough to forget about email. Long enough to hold a paperback book in our hands, and listen to the swiping of one paper page against itself. I wish boys still fist-fought over girls in long dresses.

And I wish newspapers would make a comeback.

RITES OF PASSAGE

There are rites of passage in a boy's life, benchmarks that define who he is and who he'll become. These little moments propel him into manhood, so to speak.

For instance: learning to swim is one such rite. I learned to swim with a pair of Coast-Guard-issue water wings. At the time, my dog paddled beside me in the water. We were then asked to leave the public pool

Another rite of passage: building something. A deck, a treehouse, a birdhouse. It doesn't matter what, as long as the boy uses a hammer and bleeds during the process. At which moment, he should be taught how to properly swear. And, in such scenarios, all swear words may be used except the F-word. If you have to ask why, you live above the Mason-Dixon line.

More on cussing properly: you must draw out the words into multiple syllables. For example: "shee-yet!" or "suh-hum bee-itch!" or "Gow-wad day-yum-eet to hay-ell!" And my personal favorite — well, never mind that.

Where I grew up, hunting is the biggest event a

boy's life will ever undergo. It doesn't matter what the boy's first kill is, as long as he kills it dead. Snagging a duck, deer, turkey, or squirrel, are all acceptable reasons to skip school. And skinning a squirrel is like learning your ABC's.

And then there's fishing.

Catching a first fish, is nothing short of religious, no matter what the boy's actual denomination. And, it should be noted that Methodists react differently than Baptists during this rite of passage.

When a Methodist sees his boy catch a large mouth bass, he takes a ceremonial swig from a pocket flask, then passes it to his friend. When a Baptist sees his son catch a fish, he too takes a swig. Except, he's been doing it all day. He's probably already drunk.

Regardless of denomination, if you're lucky enough to see a boy catch his first fish, the only acceptable reaction is to pretend the boy has won four state lotteries at once. This is the only instance in a man's life where screaming and giggling are permitted. Promptly followed by urination on a nearby tree to complete the ceremony.

I remember my first fish. I was five, and I caught it on Grandaddy's bamboo fishing rod. My grandfather insisted I fish with that antique piece of difficultry until I caught my first. It was a bumbling device compared to newer fishing poles, with an old corroded reel. "It's poetic," said Grandaddy. "To catch your first fish on a bamboo rod. Fiberglass poles are an abomination. You'll thank me when you get older."

I caught a rainbow trout. I still have the photograph – somewhere.

Thank you, Grandaddy.

Another wonderful occasion in a boy's life is his first memorized joke. Not a knock-knock joke, mind you. Those are ridiculous. I'm talking about a real zinger, told from start to finish, with a punchline so hard-hitting it's followed by a mushroom cloud.

My first joke was one my father taught to me. It's about three men sitting at a bar. Like most jokes are.

One man says to the group, "Fellas, have you ever said something by accident?"

Another man answers, "Yessir, just the other day, I meant to ask a woman directions and I accidentally said, 'Would you like to marry me?'"

Another man answered, "I did the same thing the other day. I ended up telling a beautiful woman, 'My, my, you have the bluest of bosoms I've ever seen."

The final man chimes in, "Well, that makes me feel better fellas. Just this morning, I meant to ask my wife to pass the sugar, instead I accidentally said, 'you've ruined my life you miserable bitch.'"

I'd have my father's friends in stitches.

They'd make me tell it a second time.

Sometimes a third.

Occasionally, a fourth.

Once, my mother caught me telling that joke. I didn't go to the bathroom right for a whole month thereafter.

Any discussion about boyhood also demands a mention of tobacco. Now, I don't smoke. I know how terrible tobacco is. But, I feel like I should remind folks it's a part of our history, and it's certainly a piece of my family's history, too.

Just before he died, my depraved ninety-seven-year-old great-great-uncle told me, "My advice to young people is, smoke all you want kids. You're going to lose your teeth and die anyway. No go get your uncle Bill a pack of smokes, son."

The pantry in my grandparent's house used to have labels on the shelves that read "Flour, Sugar, Baking Soda, Salt, Coffee." And way over on the left, "Cigarettes."

My grandparents smoked for most of their lives. And when people asked Grandaddy if he smoked, he'd usually answer, "No sir, I don't smoke, it's the cigarette that does all the smoking. I just breathe."

And you wonder why I'm a smart-ass?

I recall my first cigarette, behind our barn, it was a Chesterfield. It nearly killed me. I remember chewing my first mouthful of Red Man too, which I accidentally swallowed. I made a complete spectacle of myself at the ballgame and had to be dragged off the playing field by my cleats.

Moving right along.

The next life-ceremony for a boy is kissing a girl. That's one of the biggest rites of passage there is. And, there isn't a single male reading this who doesn't remember the events that led up to his first kiss. I can even remember what kind of shoes I was wearing for crying out loud.

Deck shoes. Brown.

The first kiss is more important than all the other bases in the idiomatic ballgame of sex. The kiss is innocent. It's pure. It launches the child out of the dugout and onto the playing field. For a boy, it's the kiss that changes a him from an undeclared major, into a bachelor looking to earn his degree.

Let's see. What else? Other American rites of passage that I've left out are: a first cup of coffee, learning to drive a car, graduating, buying a car, getting a job, buying a house, accruing debt, paying off student loans, opening an IRA, and becoming a fifty-year-old working stiff.

A more modern rite of passage is having your bank account hacked. Which is an even more meaningful experience when the offender runs off to Miami and buys two-thousand-dollars worth of Domino's pizzas with your money. I'm serious as a double bypass about that one.

One rite of passage I've been saving until last, is when a boy opens his first beer. Not drinking a first beer. The actual crack of the bottle, the hiss of the bottle cap, which is very different.

See, when a boy *opens* his first beer, it means that he intends to *drink* it. That's a very different thing than taking baby-sips from Daddy's longneck.

My first beer was consumed on a blistering hot night. I was camping with several friends in the woods near my home. I was fourteen.

My friend, Andrew, had come into possession of two entire cases. Which is a wonder. I'm not sure how someone with his babyface came by such a blessing. And, as if that wasn't impressive enough, Andrew somehow managed to carry heavy camping gear, a tent, food, water, and two heavy beer-cases miles through the woods.

It was marvelous. I'd tasted beer many times

before, but I'd never actually pretended to enjoy a full one.

At first sip, I wasn't particularly crazy about the taste. However, after two cans, it was the most delicious thing I'd ever allowed my liver the pleasure of meeting.

The next thing that happened was I became unrestrained and began to hum to myself. I found it difficult to say people's names without making a hideous hissing sound, much like a tire with a slow leak.

After my third beer, I was sobbing like a newborn. I still can't remember what exactly I cried about, but I know it had something to do with the World Series.

The thing about drunk boys: when one starts crying, they all do. Ten inebriated adolescents followed my lead, one by one. We cried for nearly an hour.

Andrew, in a charitable attempt to save the party, removed a large bottle of whiskey from his backpack.

"This is what we need," said Andrew, wiping his eyes. "My daddy says this stuff makes sadness and money-problems go away."

It sounded reasonable enough.

We popped the top off, passed it around the campfire, and nipped like we would with extra-sweet tea. I took a smaller sips than everyone else. I didn't care for the flavor. One boy noticed and shouted, "The little baby's afraid to latch on to his mama's titty. Come on you wussy, take a real swig!"

I've cleaned up the boy's language considerably because my mother reads these things.

Anyhow, that's the last thing I remember hearing before the world turned into a puddle of black licorice.

The next morning, I awoke to a curious nudging on

the seat of my pants. I flipped onto my back and was greeted by a red heifer who stood staring at me. I staggered to my feet, careful not to let my head roll off my shoulders. When I arrived back at our smoldering campsite, the boys were sprawled in the dirt like fallen soldiers among the beer cans.

I kicked Andrew with my boot.

He moaned, "What do you want?"

"Andrew, it's almost one in the afternoon, we need to get back, or they'll send the search parties out for us."

He let out another groan and curled into the fetal position. Then he sucked his thumb.

"Andrew." I nudged him again. "Get up or we'll be on the front page of the newspaper."

He finally peeled himself off the ground. Andrew and I walked home, lazily through the woods, meandering in a zig-zag pattern. The mile-long walk seemed like a forty-mile hike uphill. I was more thirsty than I've ever been in all my life, and it felt like an elf with muddy feet had danced all over my tongue.

When we got to my front porch, my mother greeted us with a solemn face. "Late night?" she asked with folded arms.

"Yes ma'am," I said.

Andrew burped.

Mother shook her head at us.

Andrew burped again, only louder. And this one seemed to amuse him.

Without saying a word, my mother rallied us into the kitchen, and fed us the fattiest breakfast Crisco would allow. She served us hot mugs of coffee, and bacon cut so thick I'm not certain it was legal. After our stomachs were sufficiently weighted down with animal fat, we told her what happened.

She just listened to our explanations without answering. Then, she stared at me and said, "Well, I'm disappointed in you."

"What about me?" hiccuped Andrew.

"I expected this of *you*."

That made Andrew's lower lip start to quiver.

She turned and left the room without uttering another syllable. And, as far as I can remember, my mother and I have never spoken of that day again. And I've done all I'm able not to make her sad again.

Thus, that's what real rites of passage look like. They're not pretty. In fact, sometimes they're ugly as sin. Whether you like it or not, it's what makes boys who they are.

Like my uncle once said, "Boys are just little shits who like to pee outdoors, hate underpants, and are proud of bodily functions."

He's not altogether wrong. Boys are like that. What else can fortify the boyish soul? What else will turn him into a fifty-year-old working stiff with a mortgage and two herniated discs?

Fishing and beer.

That's what.

ME IN MY OWN WORDS

As a child, I liked to write. I filled up notebooks with tales of the high-seas, shameless vixens, and steamy scenarios combining both of the aforementioned. My fifth grade teacher found one of my notebooks and scanned through it. She told me I wrote with too many commas, and encouraged me to pursue a career in construction work.

That, old, woman, never, liked, me.

Years later, I learned my teacher had left the school. She took a job at the Piggly Wiggly as a cashier. I went to visit the old girl, to show her the man I'd grown into.

She seemed genuinely glad to see me. And I was just as glad to find her wearing that red apron for a living. After visiting for a few minutes, I realized something I'd never noticed before. Beneath her hardshell exterior was a regular lady, working from nine to five for pennies. She was doing the best she could with her life. Just like me.

Before I left, she asked me what kind of work I did.

At the time, I worked in construction.

SEAN DIETRICH

Sean Dietrich is a writer, humorist, and novelist, known for his commentary on life in the American South. His humor and short fiction appear in various publications throughout the Southeast, including South Magazine, *the* Tallahassee Democrat, Wired Magazine, Food Network Blog, Outdoors Magazine, *and he is a member of the NWU. His first short story was published during childhood, in a hometown journal newspaper. Since then, he's pursued his literary interests authoring four novels, writing humor, and short stories.*

An avid sailor and fisherman, when he's not writing, he spends much of his time aboard his sailboat (The S.S. Squirrel), *riding the Gulf of Mexico, along with his coonhound, Ellie Mae.*

FOR MORE STORIES, OR TO CONTACT SEAN, VISIT:
WWW.SEANOFTHESOUTH.COM

Made in the USA
Las Vegas, NV
16 November 2022

59501146R00090